AF484681

This Book Belongs To A Very Brave Kid:

A new word has entered your world,
And feelings inside have swirled.

But you're braver than brave,
Like a hero, you'll save,
The day as your story is told.

You might feel mad, sad, or upset,
These emotions are normal, don't fret.

It's okay to cry,
Or to sometimes ask why,
Sharing feelings will help you, I bet.

You might wonder what happens from here
And it's okay if you have some fear.

There'll be visits galore,
To the hospital door,
But the doctors and nurses are near.

The healers have medicine to share,
To help your body repair.

Some days you might ache,
Or feel like you'll break,
But your spirit will guide you with care.

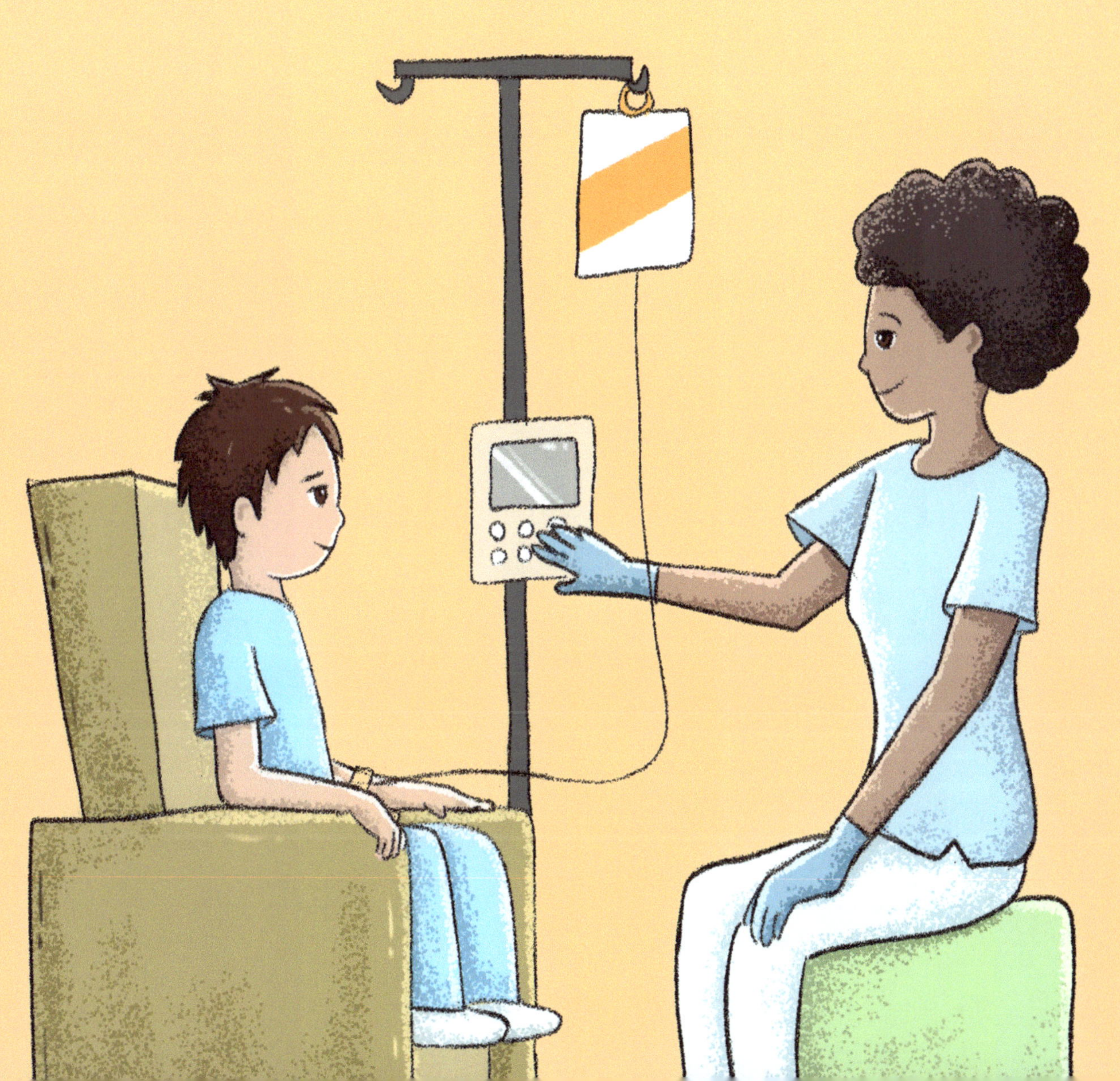

Your hair might decide to go,
But, you have so much more to show.

It's just for a while,
So keep your bright smile,
New hair will soon start to grow.

Some days you'll have tests and scans,
They're part of the doctors' big plans.

With each step that you take,
The progress you'll make,
As you conquer this challenge that stands.

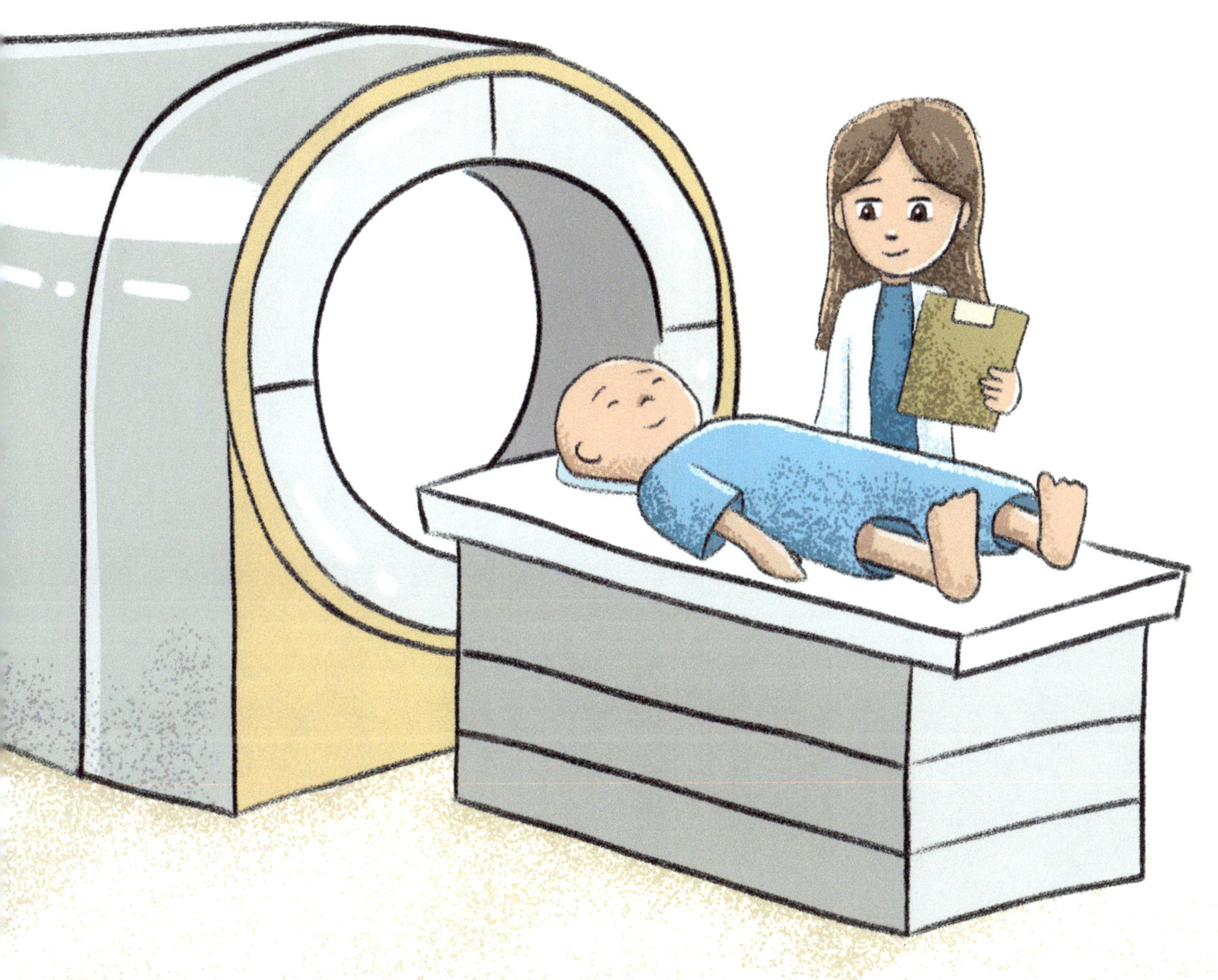

On days when you're feeling quite low,
Find things that will help your mood grow.

Read a book, sing a song,
Or just rest all day long,
It's okay to take life slow.

The warmth of your loved ones is near,
A blanket of comfort, so dear.

You are never alone,
So let it be shown,
Together, we fight away fear.

Each day brings you closer to health,
To playtime and laughter, you've felt.

Of friendships and fun,
Of races you've won,
And dreams that you've made for yourself.

So hold on to hope each day,
You are a hero in every way.

You're courageous and bold,
With a heart of pure gold,
And nothing can stand in your way!